Rush Limbaugh: The Life and Legacy of the Conservative Political Commentator Behind America's Most Popular Radio Show

By Charles River Editors

Rush Limbaugh and President Donald Trump

About Charles River Editors

Charles River Editors provides superior editing and original writing services across the digital publishing industry, with the expertise to create digital content for publishers across a vast range of subject matter. In addition to providing original digital content for third party publishers, we also republish civilization's greatest literary works, bringing them to new generations of readers via ebooks.

Sign up here to receive updates about free books as we publish them, and visit Our Kindle Author Page to browse today's free promotions and our most recently published Kindle titles.

Introduction

Gage Skidmore's picture of Rush Limbaugh in 2019

"Greetings, conversationalists across the fruited plain, this is Rush Limbaugh, the most dangerous man in America, with the largest hypothalamus in North America, serving humanity simply by opening my mouth, destined for my own wing in the Museum of Broadcasting, executing everything I do flawlessly with zero mistakes, doing this show with half my brain tied behind my back just to make it fair because I have talent on loan from…God. Rush Limbaugh. A man. A legend. A way of life." – Rush Limbaugh, 1991

With the advent of several controversial social movements in subsequent decades, a non-traditional style of editorial persona began to take control of the news machinery in America.

The weighing of ideas gave way to exclusive promotion of a specific world view, and the omission of all opposition within a devotee's range of hearing. The general population, the branches of government, and the media entered an era of divisiveness as cable television and talk radio altered the equation by which we once interacted. These important social movements of the mid-20th century, intended to enhance the status of marginalized groups, factionalized the nation in the process. New battle lines between race, gender, and political ideology brought about a similarly fragmented group of media organizations, each catering to those sharing its worldview. Finessed shadings of mutual discussion were banished as opposing arguments were negated entirely, bringing about the current era of hyperpartisanship.

In place of the 20th century's traditional news companies, a drum beat of opinion, beaten so consistently and loudly into the public consciousness that its contents became accepted as truth, was coupled with an endless search for converts. MSNBC and CNN took up the banner for the moderate-to-liberal aspects of the nation, while organizations such as PBS strove to maintain a hold on the center. As counterparts to the liberal narrative, the Tea Party, Fox News, and NOW found their own anchors. President Donald Trump spoke for the extreme conservatives, moving the central ideology significantly to the right. This movement included an espousal of isolationism and a period of "tough love" in terms of law enforcement, the economy and global relationships.

Charismatic presidents and fierce resistance have always existed together, but as the news media broke into disparate engines of political and social influence, new faces were needed, each emblematic of his or her own "congregation." The American right found the voice it needed in the supremely gifted Rush Hudson Limbaugh III. A Missourian with a lifelong love of radio, Limbaugh possessed an unmatchable rhetorical reflex, a well-informed sense of each argument's gist, and a flair for the politically incorrect. The humor, glibly delivered, was associated with sensitivities of the boomer generation's canon of cultural symbols. Once crowned as the champion of the right, Limbaugh went on to man the most popular radio talk show in America for over three decades. Such was the allure of his particular brand of on-air theater that his enemies are, by their own admission, still captivated and unable to look away. The more outrageous the style, the more compelling became the need to listen. Limbaugh eventually stood out from the radio's iconic influencers to such a degree that his sway over actual legislative and executive process made him an influential shaper of the national attitude.

Limbaugh's radio extravaganza acts much like a restrictive social network itself, with informal pressure exerted upon listeners to conform. With other opinions excluded, the audience is given a "heightened sense" of being in the majority. Liberals, at the moment less galvanized, have become intimidated and less settled in their own beliefs, while a large component of conservative Americans, perceiving themselves as unheard and railroaded into a failed social philosophy against their will, have simmered with resentment against what was branded by many on the right as social elitism. The offenders could be found among the upper industrial classes, prominent academic institutions, high-rent neighborhoods of blue-bloods exploiting their economic advantage, and progressive activists intent on the establishment of a futuristic order based on a speculative vision. For millions of people, Rush Limbaugh offered just the right voice to rail against the forces that angered these conservatives.

Rush Limbaugh: The Life and Legacy of the Conservative Political Commentator Behind America's Most Popular Radio Show chronicles how Limbaugh rose to his place of prominence and created a media empire, and the various controversies that have made him one of the most polarizing people in America. Along with pictures of important people, places, and events, you will learn about Rush like never before.

A Passion for Radio

"Most people's historical perspective begins with the day of their birth." – Rush Limbaugh

From colonial era pamphleteers to advanced communication technologies of the 21st century, local and national news media outlets have been essential, not only for providing information on current events, but as a means of influence over social and political attitudes. Compared to a time in which election speeches, important declarations, and voting results were released to the public over extended periods, modern communication systems have rendered the passing of information as virtually instantaneous. As formality in political speech waned, the public became able to interact with the process, and to ally with charismatic figures representing likeminded ideologies in the same manner as do religious denominations.

The talk radio giant of the late 20th century is not without ancestors. Had Paul Revere been granted access to modern communication, the media phenomenon would undoubtedly have occurred far earlier. Thanks to the advent of radio, some pioneers were able to employ a variation of evangelism's style over the airwaves, as practiced by healer Aimée Semple McPherson before her famous disappearing act, and Father Charles Coughlin, who developed a regular audience of millions. Perhaps an even more relatable individual is Western-style satirist Will Rogers, who took up a 15-minute slot during the early 20th century to provide a clever and rambling commentary on people and events of the day. The mutual contribution to political thought had not yet been entirely dismantled by the time of Rogers' tenure in the news, and his charm lay in the fact that no subject or public leader was untouchable. In a sense, he shared in the archetype of the modern media pastor.

Father Coughlin

Will Rogers

That said, Rogers' era of civility and information-sharing could not have foreseen the future brand of vulgarity, insults, and one-sided information sharing by which hearts were later won in the social network era. The increasing informality of American speech, a blurring of the generation gap, and a growing suspicion of denominational religion gave voiceless aspects of the population an opportunity to vent in any manner they might choose.

Jeff Schechtman, author of *The Mouth That Roared*, has argued that the riveting, quasi-religious personalities were facilitated by the earlier disc jockey. Perhaps from a sense of boredom, several began speaking to their audiences, and they understandably became enamored with the unexpectedly eager and loyal response. The advent of talk radio, Schechtman claimed, has been historically based on "codes of tribal identity, grievances, and scorn." The representation of fervent collective beliefs bloomed into an empire of big business, for some as an opportunity, and for others as an addiction. At the helm of the cable networks and prominent radio corporations was an "unparalleled group of personalities who thrived on an atmosphere that they helped drive - personal and political divisiveness." In time, every political camp was searching for a one-in-a-million talent to place before a microphone around the clock. Segments of society, each with its own list of complaints regarding tangible concerns, joined in the hunt through its corresponding news organizations.

Rush Hudson Limbaugh III was born on January 12, 1951 in the midst of these technological advances and would come of age in an era when people were accustomed to hearing news founded on the original concept of good ideas clashing in the crucible of debate in order to create a mutually developed solution. From this ongoing process, it became possible for every contributor's work to be evident in the outcome. A general state of balanced reporting was set apart from editorial news, delivered by a designated staff member.

Limbaugh was born into a family of military and legal elites in Cape Girardeau, Missouri. His father, Rush Hudson Limbaugh, Jr., served as a prominent conservative attorney and had fought in the Pacific as a fighter pilot during the Second World War. His mother, Mildred Carolyn Armstrong Limbaugh, hailed from Searcy, Arkansas and was considered the First Lady of Cape Girardeau. This was a prestigious social position well-known to those of the traditional South. One of Rush's uncles served as a federal judge in the Reagan administration, and his paternal grandfather was named the U.S. Ambassador to India under President Dwight Eisenhower. Sprinkled throughout the family tree were successful lawyers. The name of Rush was first bestowed on Limbaugh's grandfather, Rush Hudson Limbaugh, Sr., in tribute to a family member whose maiden name was Rush. Rush's younger brother David Limbaugh currently works as a conservative syndicated columnist, is an expert on law and politics, and has authored seven *New York Times* bestselling books.

Rush Limbaugh, Sr.

Gage Skidmore's picture of David Limbaugh

The future radio star's individualism was on full display by an early age. School held no fascination for the young boy, but the radio was a constant source of passion. Limbaugh claims to have decided his intended career from the age of eight-years-old, but not surprisingly, his father had an entirely different agenda mapped out for his son, and that vision required a high performance level in academics. Rush's response was that "the guy on the radio's having fun…he's not going to some room having to learn to paste."[1]

As time passed, Limbaugh was increasingly "viewed as a rebel"[2] by the family tree, but his aspirations were not totally ignored. At the age of nine, he received the gift of a Remco Caravelle, a toy radio able to transmit on AM frequencies up to a distance of 500 feet. Hiding out in his bedroom to play DJ, he later recalled that "the quality was horrible, but I was on the radio."[3]

---

[1] Biography, Rush Limbaugh – www.biography.com/media-figure/rush-limbaugh
[2] Biography

During his high school years, Limbaugh was an avid football player, but radio remained foremost in his thoughts. By 1967, at the age of 16, he was working his first job at the local studios of KGMO-AM. The station was co-owned by his father, but he did not use the family name. Working before and after school each weekday, he used the on-air alias of Rusty Sharpe after searching through the telephone book for a name that best suited him. His propensity for controversy was already apparent, but conflicts with the station management were carefully avoided with parental monitoring.

After graduating from Cape Central High School in 1969, Rush opted to enlist in the military rather than go on to college, the preference of his parents. However, the application that would have likely sent him to Vietnam was rejected due to the discovery of a pilonidal cyst, a condition affecting the sinuses. Thus, he reluctantly followed the urgings of his family and enrolled at Southeast Missouri State University in Cape Girardeau.

Once he went to college, his lack of interest failed to translate into a promising path forward, and he dropped out of school after only two semesters. Limbaugh later quipped, "The idea of going back to college scares me, and I didn't even go. I went to college for one year, two semesters. If you add up the total time, I probably didn't even go one semester."

Holding out little hope of a positive outcome, the Limbaugh family let their son go at last to try his hand at professional radio.

A Profession in Radio

"Being stuck is a position few of us like. We want something new but cannot let go of the old - old ideas, beliefs, habits, even thoughts. We are out of contact with our own genius. Sometimes we know we are stuck; sometimes we don't. In both cases we have to do something." – Rush Limbaugh

Limbaugh left home in 1971, first relocating to McKeesport, Pennsylvania, where he spent a brief period as a disc jockey. Released for his inability to contain his controversial nature, he went on to a station in Pittsburgh, where he operated under the name of Jeff Christie, and a larger station in Kansas City. Being fired for not conforming to station guidelines was becoming a habit. Limbaugh's boss in Kansas City at last informed him that a career in radio was unlikely to work out, and that he should go into sales where his rhetorical urges would serve him well.

Limbaugh took his boss literally, and did just that. He soon found a job as Director of Group Ticket Sales and Special Events for a major league baseball team, the Kansas City Royals. He was fortunate to be there during a World Series year, and was sometimes allowed to choose the singer for the National Anthem. His family members, who had resigned themselves to the likelihood that their son's life "was destined for failure,"[4] hoped that the new position would lead

---

to something sustainable. However, a telling incident occurred in which the young Limbaugh was to oversee a first ball ceremony for the team, but forgot to bring the ball. He asked those around him if one was available, and a great many were thrown at him from every direction. However, public duties for a sports team failed to command enough of his attention, and he resumed the search for radio positions in the East and Midwest.

In 1977, Limbaugh met and married his first wife, Roxy Maxine McNeely, a sales secretary from WHB in Kansas City. Bringing Roxy home to Cape Girardeau, the wedding was held in the United Methodist Centennial Church there, but the union lasted barely three years before Roxy requested a divorce on the grounds that there existed "no affinity between the two."[5]

By 1982, Limbaugh was back in radio, where, according to him, he truly belonged, even though his habit of being fired for controversial remarks continued as a professional regimen. However, a station in the West was drawn to his combative style, laced with sarcasm, wit, and sardonic humor. Station KFBK was set up for an abrasive brand of social and political commentary, but resident commentator Morton Downey, Jr. had gone too far and lost his audience with a "wild and offensive style."[6] Where Limbaugh's harsh cutting rhetoric was tailored with panache and wordplay, Downey's operating procedure was based on pure ugliness - even entertaining fistfights on the set, Downey referred to a local official as a "Chinaman" in the worst possible moment, and the gloves came off when he lampooned the language. Virtually forced from the station and the town, he was replaced by Limbaugh, whose rhetorical suave was a refreshing change, despite its similar propensity for cruelty. Within his first first weeks, the new show's ratings easily eclipsed Downey's, and Limbaugh finally appeared to have found a position he could not ruin through extreme behavior.

---

[4] Biography

[5] History-Biography, Rush Limbaugh, March 8, 2019 – www.history-biography.com/rush-limbaugh/

[6] Encyclopaedia Britannica, Rush Limbaugh, American Radio Personality and Author, January 8, 2020 – www.britannica.com

Alex Lozupune's picture of Downey, Jr.

In 1983, Limbaugh married Michelle Sixta, a "beautiful young college student and cheerleader at Kansas City Royals Stadium."[7] The second marriage outlasted the first by several years, but after less than a decade, Sixta asked for a divorce as well, leaving Limbaugh's romantic life floundering yet again.

Meanwhile, in 1987, the Federal Communications Commission (FCC) implemented a policy change that would pave the way for Limbaugh's no-holds-barred brand of political discourse. That year, the FCC repealed the Fairness Doctrine, which had been instituted, supporters claimed, as a way of creating an "informed public"[8] through equally balanced reporting about all

---

[7] History-Biography

sides of a controversial issue. Limbaugh later recollected that before the repeal, news journalists were required to go out among the populace to "ascertain the community."[9] Meetings with local figures such as the town librarian were held at certain intervals, and monitors were invited into the press room. A certain duration of coverage had to be devoted to local issues that according to Limbaugh interested no one. These were moved to Sunday morning slots. Monitors questioned the stations at length and devised ways by which entry barriers could be lowered for minorities. Limbaugh has since asserted that the Democrats have desired a reinstatement of the Fairness Doctrine since the Reagan years in order to stamp out talk radio. To him, this is because they are losing the media battle and want to call it off before suffering further humiliation.

The conservative slant on the Fairness Doctrine was that it was "unconstitutional"[10] at every conceivable level. A commentator, they asserted, could not be forced to espouse views contrary to his or her beliefs like a parrot, as to do so would be a violation of First Amendment rights. On the day the Fairness Doctrine was repealed, both liberal and conservative representatives were free to offer their slant on an issue, to the neglect or omission of the other and any attending evidence, and the fact that the repeal occurred so near in time to the establishments of the major radio and cable television news organizations is no accident. The breakdown of competing ideas in the same arena was never to be repaired, and Limbaugh was free to hold forth for the duration of an entire broadcast without resistance.

Also in 1987, Limbaugh's work caught the attention of Edward L. McLaughlin, a former director at ABC Radio. McLaughlin and the network wooed him away from northern California to work in New York City for ABC, where edgy news reporting was appreciated like nowhere else. True to form, Limbaugh soon had his new station at the top of the ratings.

In his recollections of McLaughlin and the early years of the talk radio era, Limbaugh observed that there was no successful syndicated programming during the day. Larry King led the charge at night, and Limbaugh was to try his particular style during similar hours. He worried that not enough of a salary had been secured in the negotiations to live in the city without anxiety, but in the end, things worked out well.

The show worked for a time without national advertisers, as there was no headquarter station in the city - if a studio didn't have a central station there, no one would touch any communications enterprise as an investment. Nevertheless, to Limbaugh's great relief, McLaughlin never asked him to tone it down or treat one subject more sensitively than another, and no policy at the station required any of the anchors to accommodate any complaints from callers.

As the show became more successful, various cities tried to buy it, often for the purpose of shelving it and thereby remove it as local competition. Los Angeles made the first offer, and

---

[8] National Geographic, August 4, 1987, CE: Fairness Doctrine Repealed
[9] Rush Limbaugh.com
[10] National Geographic

McLaughlin was tempted, but, he eventually declined. Otherwise, Limbaugh never would have been broadcast in California's largest city.

A Radio and Television Star

"Can't take sides? These were American journalists, and they can't take sides? That attitude illustrates the haughty arrogance of people in the news business." – Rush Limbaugh

The Rush Limbaugh Show debuted on August 1, 1988, and within five years, the three-hour program had become the most popular talk show in radio history. Limbaugh claimed that many people believe the Clinton administration was the reason for the show's rising popularity, but Limbaugh's realm had grown from 56 to 600 stations before Clinton was elected. The format of the program has scarcely changed since its inception, with an opening monologue in the style of late night television broadcasts. Satirical advertising and standard comedy sketches are mixed with a comprehensive discussion of the current news. Through the years, leading political figures, including George W. Bush and Colin Powell, have appeared as guests. Most attractive of all, however, was the "heavy use of Limbaugh himself."[11]

The establishment of the show was well-timed, as the political highpoint of the Civil Rights Movement was still fresh in the public's mind and by no means complete in its aspirations. The feminist movement was well under way, and the subject of environmentalism was creeping gradually into the public consciousness. Since Limbaugh held ferociously anti-liberal views on these movements, the airwaves were fertile ground for an ideological battle.

In the midst of the Clinton administration, the *National Review* was the first to elevate Limbaugh as a figurehead of conservative opposition. He harbored a special distaste for Clinton and his wife, Hillary, even beyond that of Barack Obama. As a reward for his tortuous portrayals of the soon-to-be impeached Clinton, Republican lawmakers presented Limbaugh with the title of Honorary Member of Congress.

Along with his criticism of the president, Limbaugh's penchant for racial commentary perceived as humiliating and abusive, his ready arsenal of "uncomfortable comments"[12] about women, and his staunchly pro-death penalty stance all made him a controversial national figure, but he found a giant audience of willing listeners who were clearly weary of the mainstream's adherence to any sense of national decorum. Inevitably, as his stature rose among his devotees, Limbaugh became more emboldened and controversial, seemingly immune to any repercussions from an ordinarily grateful network. The growing flock of followers, fondly known as "dittoheads,"[13] formed such an avid listening and caller base that the most prestigious of guests served as straight men and sidekicks for the main attraction, Limbaugh himself. Vastly

---

[11] Encyclopaedia Britannica
[12] History-Biography
[13] Encyclopaedia Britannica

surpassing the ratings and audience of any other such format on the air, Limbaugh let loose his full ideological assault on American groups otherwise accustomed to civility from all other quarters.

Among the largest of his targets were women in the feminist movement. Limbaugh himself widely used and popularized the term "feminazi" and wielded it against organizations promoting equal job opportunities and uniform pay scales for women in the job market. The term, which belittled the status of females as partners in full standing within relationships or business ventures, was defined at length by Limbaugh:

> "I prefer to call the most obnoxious feminists what they really are: feminazis. Tom Hazlett, a good friend who is an esteemed and highly regarded professor of economics at the University of California at Davis, coined the term to describe any female who is intolerant of any point of view that challenges militant feminism. I often use it to describe women who are obsessed with perpetuating a modern-day holocaust: abortion. There are 1.5 million abortions a year, and some feminists almost seem to celebrate that figure. There are not many of them, but they deserve to be called feminazis.

> "A feminazi is a woman to whom the most important thing in life is seeing to it that as many abortions as possible are performed. Their unspoken reasoning is quite simple. Abortion is the single greatest avenue for militant women to exercise their quest for power and advance their belief that men aren't necessary. They don't need men in order to be happy. They certainly don't want males to be able to exercise any control over them. Abortion is the ultimate symbol of women's emancipation from the power and influence of men. With men being precluded from the ultimate decision-making process regarding the future of life in the womb, they are reduced to their proper, inferior role. Nothing matters but me, says the feminazi. My concerns prevail over all else. The fetus doesn't matter, it's an unviable tissue mass."

Over the years, Limbaugh drew a satirical connection between "liberated" women and "ugly duckling" syndrome The women's movement, he quipped on air, allowed "unattractive women easier access to the mainstream."[14] This legion of females seeking a way out of the patriarchal tradition was connected to the Democratic Party, a group of addled and "henpecked" men who "can't wait to fund every abortion in the world."[15] Limbaugh has continued to assert that the feminist movement is based on the "given an inch, take a mile" philosophy, and that in getting what they want, the members are never satisfied. Referring to an article in the *Washington Post* written by Professor of Sociology Suzanna Danuta Waters, he has insisted that feminists have achieved 90% of all they requested, including gay marriage and transgender rights, and that they

---

[14] Encyclopaedia Britannica

[15] Encyclopaedia Britannica

have successfully "corrupted and taken over the Boy Scouts."[16] And yet, he maintains, they remain unhappy. Limbaugh has ruminated out loud that the modern feminist is not "constitutionally capable of happiness."[17]

A picture of Limbaugh on *The Phil Donahue Show* in 1991

By 1992, Limbaugh was tempted to enter the political realm himself. Presidential candidate Pat Buchanan invited him to join the ticket, but he gratefully declined – after all, the confines of his studio offered protection from the political crucible, and acting as a commentator remained far more satisfying than playing the victim of public investigation and partisan scorn. Limbaugh opted instead to extend the format of his radio program to television. It was housed by a format produced by Roger Ailes, the disgraced director of Fox News, who was eventually fired over sexual harassment suits.

---

[16] Rush Limbaugh.com, June 11, 2018, Feminist in Washington Post: Why Can't We Hate Men/
[17] Rush Limbaugh Show.com

Ninian Reid's picture of Ailes and Rupert Murdoch

Limbaugh's on-camera persona was as persuasive as it was on the airwaves, and the show ran for a period of four years. Viewer videos were added, and Nick Africano, an artist and actor, sought out interesting bits of information from the streets of New York. Drawing items from media and political figures was Marc Morano, a former Republican aide playing "Our Man in Washington." Morano was notorious for mocking environmental scientists in television debates by attempting to dig up scientific resistance to climate change, as well as publishing the damaging "Swiftboat" charges against John Kerry. Limbaugh could not resist including an elderly female reporter who once yelled at Bill Clinton, "Everything is going down the drain. Is that true?" She gratefully took on the occasional role as "Our Woman in Washington."

Around the start of the show's run, the topic of immigration heated up, as it would again during the Trump administration. Limbaugh argued that the Statue of Liberty was not intended to physically welcome immigrants to American shores, but to allegorically help them set an example for living in their own countries in the manner of the American model. The *Huffington Post* reported that regarding "migrants" themselves, Limbaugh once remarked that drinking water from the toilet was "a step up"[18] for such people.

---

[18] Huffpost, Rush Limbaugh – www.huffpost.com/news/topic/rush-limbaugh

Ultimately, Limbaugh decided to terminate the television show four years after its inception, owing to the one half-hour format and a weak scheduling slot in the early morning hours. Meanwhile,

In 1992, the first of Limbaugh's best-selling books was published, entitled *The Way Things Ought to Be*. Told from the type of conservative viewpoint that fans had come to expect, the publication drew a retaliatory response from the watchdog group known as Fairness and Accuracy in Reporting. They published a tome entitled *The Way Things Aren't: Rush Limbaugh's Reign of Error*, detailing a long list of what they considered his inaccuracies and fraudulent assertions.

Undeterred by such publications produced by organizations with smaller followings, Limbaugh continued to take aim at most of the hot button issues of the day. Among these were what he termed the "Imperial Congress,"[19] Anita Hill and her sexual harassment accusations against Justice Clarence Thomas, those liberals he referred to as "social utopians,"[20] and all things environmental. The content of the watchdog response was equal in sizzle, featuring a list of "100 whoppers"[21] and the most outrageous Limbaugh contradictions. Ultimately, however, *The Way Things Aren't* could not hope to compete with Limbaugh's following and thus found itself drowned out.

A more serious tome was published in 1993 by Daniel Joseph Evearitt, entitled *Rush Limbaugh and the Bible*. Attempting to dive into the source of Limbaugh's faith, Evearitt examined the underpinnings of his show and covered modern issues through a Biblical framework as viewed by a conservative informed by literalist faith. Limbaugh further infused himself into a religious-tinged political ministry by advertising David Limbaugh's *Jesus on Trial: A Lawyer Affirms the Truth of the Gospel*. Whether the religious associations are connected is unclear, but Limbaugh was inducted into the Radio Hall of Fame around the same time, and Limbaugh discussed his own return to the Christian following after admitting he found God too mysterious to take seriously as a concept in his early years. According to Limbaugh, it was only after a study of apologetics that he believed God was in front of him the whole time, and that the Scriptures had been handed down in pure form.

In 1994, Limbaugh tied the knot once again, this time to Marta Fitzgerald, an aerobics instructor. They were married in a secular ceremony at the home of Justice Clarence Thomas, who presided over the wedding. The two via the internet through a dating site catering to a high-income brand of clientele, even though Marta was married at the time.

After the wedding, she was not prone to be a social presence at their Palm Springs residence. Having received a journalism degree from the University of North Florida and an internship at

---

[19] Goodreads.com, The Way Things Ought to Be, - www.goodreads.com/book/show/543707.The _Way_Things_Ought_to_Be

[20] Goodreads.com

[21] Goodreads.com

the *Jacksonville Times-Union*, she lost money launching a magazine during the couple's early years together. She had been married three times before meeting Limbaugh, and she maintained a low profile in their public life, so much so that the two were rarely seen together. It is suggested by some that they lived in separate houses on adjoining lots at one point during their marriage, which lasted about a decade. Limbaugh announced their separation on the air, and Marta subsequently found success in real estate.

Soon after marrying Fitzgerald, Limbaugh's next book, *See I Told You So*, was released. Addressing his favorite topics, from religion to whether a woman is always or ever right, the book flew to the top of the bestseller lists, much like the others. Goodreads advertised *See I Told You So* as being authored by this "harmless little fuzzball"[22] who delights in being called "the most dangerous man in America."[23]

1994 was important for Limbaugh's on-air and behind-the-scenes work for the Republican Party. He was largely credited with helping the party win both houses of Congress in that election by energizing his vast army of listeners. Limbaugh and his media format had by this time eclipsed the political pundit and legislator environment for bringing about change within the electoral structure. In barely half a decade, he had "reshaped the political landscape with his entertaining and informative brand of conservatism."[24] In addition, he had repositioned AM radio as a principal media presence in American culture.

As a celebrity, Limbaugh received numerous invitations for television appearances as himself and various fictional characters. In 1995, he appeared in *Forget Paris*, a romantic comedy starring Billy Crystal and Debra Winger. Soon after, he appeared on *The Drew Carey Show*, the host of which was an avid sportsman, former U.S. Marine, and staunch libertarian.

Rush Limbaugh, Sr. died in 1996 at the age of 104 and was well-noted as the oldest practicing attorney in the United States. Limbaugh's mother died four years later. In tending to her during her last days, Limbaugh moved the entire radio show to Cape Girardeau and broadcast the full three hours from her home. Callers were forwarded to a local phone line, and business went forward as usual.

Following the loss of his grandfather and mother, central issues continued to be discussed on his radio show, while sporadic skirmishes between left and right continued to thrill audiences of both camps as lighter entertainment. The release of a one-man stage play, *Rush Limbaugh in Night School,* titillated anti-Rush cult audiences. Charlie Varon's "complex tale of Limbaugh's downfall"[25] utilized 20 peripheral characters as the pundit is placed within every situation he opposed in real life. In one scene, he purportedly plays Othello in blackface while yearning for a

---

[22] Goodreads.com, See, I Told You So, Rush Limbaugh – www.goodreads.com/book/show/117373.See_I_Told_You_So

[23] Goodreads.comj

[24] KFGW, Rush Limbaugh

[25] Amy Martin, Review: Rush Limbaugh in Night School – www.moonlady.com/review-rush-limbaugh-in-night-school/

1960s feminist left-wing radical who is on the run from the FBI.

As this suggests, liberal Americans had their own stars, such as comedian Al Franken. As Limbaugh parodies proliferated, Franken's book, *Rush Limbaugh is a Big Fat Idiot and Other Observations*, made the biggest splash on bookshelves. Other right-wing characters appear, and the book was inspired by the earlier rise of Speaker of the House Newt Gingrich, but Franken could not help but place Limbaugh squarely at the center.

Franken

The impeachment of President Bill Clinton was initiated in October 1998, and Limbaugh became a key figure behind the scenes, despite having no specific role in the actual proceedings. Some of Limbaugh's shows as recently as 2019 discussed what he believed were the major differences between the impeachments of Clinton and Trump, typically in an effort to demonstrate the deeper seriousness of Clinton offenses.

Limbaugh threw an equal amount of passion into the George W. Bush campaign in 2000, and the only threat to Limbaugh's tenure as America's leading talk show host came as a result of several bouts with poor health in 2001. That year, he announced on the show that he had gone "100% totally deaf,"[26] a condition that eliminated television and music from his life.

---

[26] Annika Reed, Maria Puente

Adjustments had to be made for responding to calls or on-site conversation. It had all occurred, he said, over the space of three months. Limbaugh was diagnosed with AIED, auto-immune inner ear disease, and medications had thus far failed. In time, a portion of his hearing was restored through the insertion of a cochlear implant on one side. Encouraged, he underwent the same procedure on the other side, and claims to have experienced enormous improvement, leading to a virtual restoration of his hearing. To the listening audience, he concluded, "Coming from total deafness, it is miraculous. How can you not believe in God?" [27]

The hiring of Rush Limbaugh as a sports commentator was not on the face of it such an outlandish idea. A follower of numerous sports and a former football player, his ability to speak off the cuff should have made for an entertaining feature in professional sports. ESPN hired Limbaugh in 2003 and assigned him to weekly NFL games, including for a Philadelphia Eagles football game. All was going well until Limbaugh suddenly steered the subject of a black quarterback into a discussion of race politics and liberal media biases. From the booth, he downplayed Eagles quarterback Donovan McNabb's ability, remarking, "I don't think he's been that good from the get-go. I think what we've had here is a little social concern in the NFL. I think the media has been very desirous that a black quarterback do well. They're interested in black coaches and black quarterbacks doing well. I think there's a little hope invested in McNabb and he got a lot of credit for the performance of his team that he really didn't deserve."

For many spectators, sports represents a momentary escape from political squabbles and social rancor, and the sudden injection of controversial comments caused problems. Limbaugh resigned from ESPN in short order, before he could be fired, and the color analyst position for the NFL was given instead to comedian Dennis Miller, who at times experienced similar troubles navigating political and social issues.

A second round of health setbacks landed Limbaugh in trouble with the law. In 2006, he was placed under arrest and charged with illegally obtaining prescription drugs. As a means of doing this, he was said to have "doctor shopped"[28] to amass an ongoing supply of opioid painkillers. He announced on the show that his addiction had been a problem for some time, and that a botched back surgery to relieve years of back pain was the culprit.

The investigation into Limbaugh began with a report in the *National Enquirer* surrounding a housekeeper's allegations that the radio star abused Oxycontin and other painkillers. Naturally, the accusation was a threat to Limbaugh's on-air diatribes against illegal drug use and abuse, given that he had previously expressed little compassion for drug users. In fact, he had repeatedly insisted that drug offenders should all be "convicted…[and] sent up."[29] Drug use was among the issues Limbaugh constantly brought up to lambast President Clinton, and his own

---

[27] Annika Reed, Maria Puente

[28] Encyclopaedia Britannica

[29] CBS News, April 28, 2006, Rush Limbaugh Arrested on Drug Charges – www.cbsnews.org/news/rush-limbaugh-arrested-on-drug-charges/

confession required a fair amount of finessed hairsplitting and at least mock humility.

Limbaugh turned himself in and was charged with concealing information to obtain prescriptions. Bail was set at $3,000, a pittance for one of his stature. In a seizure of his medical records and a search of his residence, overlapping prescriptions were found, indicating that he had received approximately 2,000 painkillers over a six-month period through a pharmacy near his Palm Beach mansion. After he pled not guilty, the court offered to dismiss charges after a period of 18 months if Limbaugh was able to comply with the court's guidelines, including rehab. No further action was taken outside of a $30,000 payment to the State of Florida for investigative costs. Limbaugh continued to deny that he doctor-shopped, and he remained a free man.

Fox News' answer to Jon Stewart's *Daily Show* on Comedy Central was released under the title *The ½ Hour News Hour,* premiering in 2007. In part inspired by the format of *Saturday Night Live,* the program was originally titled *This Just In.* Although not a member of the ongoing cast, Limbaugh appeared in a notable sketch as a fictitious president with Ann Coulter as his vice president. One of the major rating organizations described the launch as "Fox News' failed attempt to create their own Daily Show."[30]

Although *The ½ Hour News Hour* failed in a relatively short time, the year was a productive one for Limbaugh's image, as he was nominated for a Nobel Peace Prize. By 2008, his media empire was powerful enough to insulate devoted listeners from alternate worldviews, simply by the dimensions of his on-air presence and their increased allegiance. As an underlying feature, Limbaugh strove to cause a mistrust of alternate media sources through a system of "balkanization"[31] with which to blot out the concept of two-sided news. By causing a state of single-mindedness in a "far-flung and disparate nation," self-perceived have-nots were aroused to a state of revolution, financed by multi-millionaires behind the scenes with whom they had little in common. Officials within the Republican Party embraced this movement so much that Limbaugh became an important part of the vetting of potential candidates.

From the beginning of *The Rush Limbaugh Show*, the production team has remained almost entirely unbroken. Surrounding Limbaugh on every working day is producer James Golden, known to the radio audience as the "beloved Bo Snerdely."[32] Other mainstays of the studio are Engineer Mike Maimone and Chief of Staff "Kit" Carson. Through the years, awards from conservative bastions have constantly been given to Limbaugh. In 2007, he received the Award of Excellence in Media, and he has been named Man of the Year by the conservative magazine *Human Events.*

---

[30] IMDB.com, The ½ Hour News Hour – www.imdb.com/title/tt0887788/

[31] Steven Classen, Review of Echo Chamber: Rush Limbaugh and the Conservative Media Establishment by Kathlyn Hall Jamieson, Joseph N. Cappella, *Cinema Journal*, Vol. 51 no. 4 (Summer 2012) Oxford University Press

[32] Mark Davis, A Prayer for Rush Limbaugh, Feb. 4, 2020, Townhall – www.townhall.com/columnists/markdavis/2020/02/04/a-prayer-for-rush-limbaugth-n2560665

Going Too Far

"What he is talking about is the absorption of as much of the private sector by the US government as possible, from the banking business, to the mortgage industry, the automobile business, to health care. I do not want the government in charge of all of these things. I don't want this to work. So I'm thinking of replying to the guy, 'Okay, I'll send you a response, but I don't need 400 words, I need four: I hope he fails.'…So what is so strange about saying I want Barack Obama to fail if his mission is to reconstruct and reform this nation so that capitalism and individual liberty are not its foundation? I want the country to survive. I want the country to succeed." – Rush Limbaugh

Much the way the administration of Bill Clinton had fired up millions of people and boosted Limbaugh, the 2008 election of Barack Obama infused the radio host and his audience with increased fervor. The conservative champion had labored unceasingly to extend the suspense through the Democratic primaries, and in order to befuddle his liberal opponents, he recommended to his listeners that they cross over in open primaries and vote for Hilary Clinton. To facilitate this tactic, he employed voter data from North Carolina and election returns from Indiana, North Carolina, and Pennsylvania. When it was asserted by some in Ohio that it was a felony to fraudulently register as a Democrat to disrupt the primary, as Limbaugh was advocating, Leo Jennings, a spokesperson for the Ohio Attorney General, replied, "We have no intention of prosecuting Rush Limbaugh because lying through your teeth and being stupid isn't a crime."

It was Limbaugh who in the end galvanized national opposition to the new president's stimulus package, while signing a deal to remain on the radio for $400 million over eight years. In Obama's first year, Limbaugh was inducted into the National Broadcasters Association Hall of Fame.

Questions concerning Limbaugh's overall health continued in 2009, especially after he suffered at least one heart attack scare while in Hawaii. Complaining of severe chest pains, he was taken by paramedics from the Kahala Hotel and Resort to the Queen's Medical Center in Honolulu, according to station KITV. In transit, he was said to be in "serious condition."[33] Tests for a cardiac event proved negative, and he was released the following day. The onset of the incident was not a sudden one, as he later related to Fox News that he had "felt a heart attack coming on."[34]

Not surprisingly, 2010 was also spent railing against the Obama administration. On the policy side, Limbaugh denounced the president for what he saw as excessive and misplaced spending, whereas he would dismiss the ramifications of spending during the Trump administration by

---

[33] Fox News, Associated Press, Rush Limbaugh Felt 'Heart Attack Coming On', Jan. 1, 2010 – www.foxnews.com/story/rush-limbugh-felt-heart-attack-coming-on

[34] Fox News.com, Associated Press

observing, "No one is a fiscal conservative anymore."[35]

In his personal attacks, he led the charge for the "birther" conspiracy, claiming that the birth certificate offered by Obama was a forgery and that his real place of birth was Kenya. Pushing the theory that Obama was indeed a Muslim and anti-American activist, the venom spilled over into racial insults and matters involving the Obama family.

On the other side, Limbaugh parodies continued to appear among various liberal sources. Chicago's Second City, an improvisational theater troupe, produced a theater piece entitled *Rush Limbaugh – The Musical*. From start to finish, the production was put together and presented in a total of 13 days, employing "different actors and different egos."[36] Characters include the Reverent Rightwing, and assassins are unable to plot against Obama after they profess love for him, including observing that "he's just the right amount of black."[37]

Unfazed and reveling in the fight, Limbaugh went on to serve as a judge for the Miss America pageant in Las Vegas. Along the way, he received the William F. Buckley Award for Media Excellence. The Conservative Political Action Conference, "the most influential gathering of conservatives in the world,"[38] granted Limbaugh the Defender of the Constitution Award.

Also in 2010, Limbaugh married for the fourth time, this time to Kathryn Adams, an event planner from Massachusetts with a direct ancestral lineage to President John Adams. The couple had met six years prior while she was running golfer Gary Player's celebrity charity golf tournament, in which Limbaugh participated as a player. The "lavish 2010 wedding"[39] included a performance by Elton John for a $1 million dollar fee, and it was followed by a Mexican honeymoon aboard Limbaugh's Gulfstream jet. Limbaugh and his wife went on to collaborate on a series of popular children's books centered on the prominent adventures of a Limbaugh-inspired character named Rush Revere. As the last name suggests, the books contain brief tales of iconic American historical events and famous figures.

With the progression of the Obama administration came a renewed tide of conservative commentary, much of which reverted to what many considered overtly racist. Limbaugh's full fire continued to be aimed at the president's legitimacy and alleged arrogance. In likening Obama to God, he quipped that neither one was in possession of a birth certificate. The difference, he said, was that "God doesn't think he's Obama."[40] Casting the Democrat as a member of the academic elite, Limbaugh constantly belittled the president's education, suggesting that he never would have made it into or out of Harvard without affirmative action. In

[35] Billy Binion, Rush Limbaugh Abandons Fiscal Conservatism, 7/18/2019 – www.reason.com/2019/07/18/rush-limbaugh-abandons-fiscal-conservatism/

[36] Rush Limbaugh – The Musical, March 4, 2010 – www.rushthemusical.blogspot.com

[37] Rush Limbaugh – The Musical

[38] American Conservative Union, CPAC, 2020 – www.cpac.conservative.org

[39] Andrea Simpson, Enquirer, Nov. 24, 2015 – www.nationalenquirer.com/celebrity/why-rush-limbaugh-no-rush-divorce-his-wick-wife

[40] AZ Quotes, Rush Limbaugh – www.azquotes.com/author/8876-Rush_Limbaugh

the introduction to his show, Limbaugh took to playing a song entitled *Barack the Magic Negro,* set to the tune of *Puff the Magic Dragon.* In another instance, he made a reference to Curious George, playing on an old, racist stereotype of blacks being unevolved humans. Likely under pressure, he issued an apology soon after, claiming not to know that Curious George was a monkey.

All the while, mocking the president's children was not out of bounds for Limbaugh. A story emerged in which Malia asked her father, "Did you plug the hole yet?"[41] This was a reference to the British Petroleum oil spill in the Gulf of Mexico, and on the air, Limbaugh satirized Malia in a high-pitched voice asking her father, "Daddy, daddy, did you shake down BP yet?"

At a time when many conservatives feared a run for office by Michelle Obama following her husband's term, the president's family purchased a beach house in Martha's Vineyard. Limbaugh immediately drew a connection to the Kennedy family, since they also lived in the vicinity. The joke seemed lighthearted in contrast to some assaults: "Gonna be so close to the Kennedys they could throw water balloons at each other."[42]

Black conservatives could rely on Limbaugh for on-air support for their projects and campaigns, but liberal and non-Christian minorities were constant targets. Louis Farrakhan, the leader of the Nation of Islam, has long been at odds with Limbaugh in matters of cultural faith and racial destiny. Limbaugh gave him the derisive nickname "Calypso Louie," a reference to Farrakhan's former career as a musician.

---

[41] Media Matters for America, Echoing Glenn Beck, Rush Limbaugh Mocks Malia Obama – www.mediamatters.org/rush-limbaugh-echoing-glenn-beck-rush-limbaugh-mocks-Malia-Obama

[42] IHeart Radio, Why Would the Obamas Buy a Doomed Beach House? Premiere Networks, August 23, 2019 - www.iheart.com/featured/rush-limbaugh/content/2019-08-23rush-limbaugh-why-would-the-obamas-buy-a-doomed-beachhouse/

Farrakhan

In the same vein, Limbaugh has often reserved special condescension for black callers. One contentious exchange ended with Limbaugh telling his black detractor to "take that bone out of your nose and call me back."[43] He asked his audience if they had ever noticed that all composite pictures of wanted criminals bore a striking resemblance to Jesse Jackson, and he claimed that Supreme Justice Sonia Sotomayor "brings a form of bigotry and racism to the court."[44]

By offering a historical reminder that the Democratic Party once consisted of plantation owners and those who owned slaves, Limbaugh has frequently conducted "a re-scripting of the civil rights movement."[45] Accompanying this historical note is the delineation between two kinds of racist offense. Limbaugh was incensed when Herman Cain, a black Tea Party activist and

---

[43] *Journal of Blacks in Higher Education*, Rush Limbaugh: The Master of Racial; Poison, No. 64 (Summer 2009), JHBE Foundation

[44] *Journal of Blacks in Higher Education*

[45] Allison Perlman, Rush Limbaugh and the Problem of the Color Line, *Cinema Journal,* Vol. 15 no. 4 (Summer 2012) University of Texas

presidential candidate, was accused of sexual harassment, but a ruthlessly stereotypical cartoon of a big-lipped Cain eating watermelon did not garner protest from the radio host. The first offense against Cain was to Limbaugh a career threatening scandal, but to protest the cartoon would have signified a bowing down to modern political correctness. As he has with other cultural movements of the latter 20th century, Limbaugh "claims the mantle of civil rights for conservatives."[46] He touts himself as able to defeat opposing liberal arguments with "half his brain tied behind his back."[47]

Whatever the result in terms of social divisiveness, Limbaugh has said that the heavy-handed white response to marches for civil rights in the Deep South during the 1960s was ideal for politically uniting the region, tightening the conservative grip on the region for decades to come. According to Limbaugh, since his idea of a conservative is the descendant of Republican anti-slavery, the conservative is also the ideological child of Martin Luther King's activism in Limbaugh's view. Liberals, on the other hand, are perpetrators of systemic racism, which they cloud over with empathetic rhetoric. Limbaugh's bottom line on liberal racism is due to the belief that they "see it"[48] in virtually every social interaction. For colorful emphasis, Limbaugh refers to the Democratic Party as "The Plantation,"[49] but he has refused to acknowledge conservative support for segregation in the early-to-mid 20th century.

Given these views, perhaps it is no surprise that Limbaugh considers black conservatives the noblest kind. Those he has promoted on the air include Clarence Thomas, J.C. Watts, Alan Keyes, and Ward Connerly.

As for history, Limbaugh has stated openly that for over a century, the institution of slavery was "not a bad thing."[50] Reminding listeners of what the white race got out of it, he cited the building of the entire South. He cautioned that he has no wish to bring slavery back to the American system, but he has insisted, "It had merits. For one thing, the streets were safer after dark."[51]

Limbaugh's explanation for Obama's victory also differs from what Democrats see as a linear evolution of tolerance and familiarity among the mainstream public. Through the eyes of Limbaugh, Obama succeeded where Jesse Jackson and Al Sharpton could not due to an artful "manipulation of white guilt."[52] Being given a seat at the feast of liberation, white America was offered a refreshing exception to the past, to enjoy a modicum, however brief, of "racial innocence."[53] To Limbaugh, Jackson and Sharpton made progress a challenge, an exercise in

---

[46] Allison Perlman

[47] Allison Perlman

[48] Allison Perlman

[49] Allison Perlman

[50] The Hollowverse, Rush Limbaugh – www.hollowverse.com/rush-limbaugh/

[51] The Hollowverse

[52] Allison Perlman

[53] Allison Perlman

defiance and righteous indignation, while Obama reshaped his campaign into a course of soothing national therapy.

If anything was able to occupy Limbaugh's time and attention as much as racial politics, it was feminism. In the 2010s, Limbaugh continued to claim that the issue was rewritten into an inauthentic protest levied by inferior females lacking sufficient sexual allure. The ideal woman, Limbaugh once joked, is "35-24-36, five foot seven, flat on top of the head, deaf mute."[54] The flat spot on the head was, he said, intended for holding a man's drink. Historically, he added, the advent of a woman's right to vote following World War I opened the floodgates of erratic emotionalism, counterproductive to sober governing. As for the modern woman, she desires the same thing as her ancestors did, and she bristles at being approached in an intimate manner due to the curse of political correctness. According to Limbaugh, the "Me Too" movement stands as a collective hysterical fit that a good romantic encounter could easily relieve.

Limbaugh's extreme comments on a woman's place in society erupted into a major controversy in February 2012, proving that "one man's controversy is another man's hot topic of the day."[55] That month, Sandra Fluke, a young law student at Georgetown University, testified before Congress on the issue of insurance and birth control. Fluke's argument was that birth control through three years of school was a heavy burden, reaching approximately $3,000. Insurance companies, she believed, had a responsibility to cover the expense as it would other medical necessities.

On his show, Limbaugh characterized Ms. Fluke as a "poor little 23-year-old university waif,"[56] adding that if she could afford three years of Georgetown, she could afford birth control, especially since it was an optional item to buy, not a medical necessity. Conservatives were buoyed by the reality that Fluke turned out to be 30, and Limbaugh's attack on her lack of sincerity spilled over into a defining moment in which he called her "a slut"[57] and "a prostitute."[58] If she were otherwise, reasoned Limbaugh, the protection of birth control would never have been needed.

Fluke was devastated and the American mainstream was shocked by the comments, to the point that Limbaugh's network lost its nerve. Despite the host offering an apology of sorts, advertisers abandoned the show in droves until they had nearly all disappeared. Of all the losses, the biggest blow came from the withdrawal of eHarmony, a science-oriented dating site, which cancelled its association "forever."[59]

---

[54] AZ Quotes

[55] Newstalk 1290.com, Limbaugh and Fluke: The Not-So-Love Story – www.newstalk.1290.com/limbaugh-and-flukethe-no-so-love-story/

[56] Newstalk 1290

[57] Newstalk 1290

[58] Newstalk 1290

[59] Frank Lake, Rush Limbaugh Fired, Weekly World News, March 6, 2012 – www.weeklyworldnews.com/headlines/44895/rush-limbaugh-fired

To the dismay of 20 million listeners, Rush Limbaugh, the champion of politically incorrect discourse, was fired. Clear Channel and its subsidiary, Prime Radio Networks, felt as though they had no choice but to end the program, even as conservatives complained that Bill Maher had committed the same offense by addressing Sarah Palin with a term that was even worse. They cried foul that the only reason he got away with it was due to his lack of need for advertisers. Outraged dittoheads felt Limbaugh was being punished for speaking the truth with a purity lacking in all other sources of information, and that his assault on Fluke was a heroic gesture to his vast base. In protest against his suspension, many burned their radios, while in some quarters, liberals gloated as President Obama announced on Air Force One that it was "a good day for freedom of speech."[60]

Recent Years

"I think it would be too easy to dismiss him as being irrelevant to the shaping of opinion in this country today. He's very smart. He does his homework. He is well-informed. And you ignore him at your peril." – Ted Koppel

It didn't take long for Limbaugh to regain his position with his network, and if anyone thought he had been chastened by his termination, he quickly demonstrated that he entertained no change in his rhetoric of anti-liberalism. He had danced too close to the line for an instant, but the playing field was unchanged, and while he felt political correctness had won the day, his resistance continued. For many, the political correctness was merely inauthentic and cowardly, but to Limbaugh, it stood as an overarching lie of liberalism, the grandest social camouflage covering centuries of hypocrisy. Ignoring for the moment that the nation's structure and processes are termed "liberal democracy," he retaliated against the term as the "antithesis of being pro-human."[61] For liberals, he declared that the experience of life is "a thing to be managed"[62] rather than something to be explored and lived to the fullest.

Throughout the last decade, Limbaugh brought several issues to the fore with greater force than he had in the past, albeit remaining somewhat careful to avoid another Sandra Fluke experience.

His defense of the Second Amendment remained loud and clear during debates over gun control, which often rise to the fore in the wake of mass shootings. The purpose of the Second Amendment, as he constantly put it, is that it exists "in case the government fails to follow the first one."[63]

The phenomenon of Black Lives Matter has been so appalling to Limbaugh that he can scarcely drum up enough humor to keep the program entertaining. When a shooting took place in

---

[60] Frank Lake

[61] IMDB, Biography, Rush Limbaugh – www.imdb.com/name/nm0510754/bio

[62] IMDB, Rush Limbaugh

[63] AZ Quotes

a major city involving a man with a long rap sheet injuring six police officers, his main contention was that residents of the building were cheering for the shooter. This, Limbaugh swore, was the legacy of Barack Obama. In such a situation, he pointed to the absurdity of believing that a red flag law or other item of legislation could have prevented the incident or similar ones. However, as he told a caller upset with his mayor's lax attitude toward enforcement, whether it's the president or the mayor, "It's tough to beat Santa Claus."[64]

One of the most unembroidered responses to the gun control crisis was offered without his usual satire. Limbaugh's take on a Bret Stephens article in the Wall Street Journal recommending repeal of the Second Amendment possessed an unusual kind of gravitas. The carefully ordered rebuttal was reliant on Limbaugh's personal sense of logic without the showmanship. The case for repealing the amendment flabbergasted the pundit to the point that he was forced to invoke the help of conservative expert Charles C.W. Cooke, who wrote a piece on the subject for the *National Review*. Stephens was an avowed conservative, but one who claimed to have never understood the conservative "fetish"[65] for guns. What Stephens failed to understand, Limbaugh observed, was "the reach that tyrannies have enjoyed"[66] over the centuries in every conceivable location. A second point Limbaugh made was that the Second Amendment was not just an amendment, but a codification of a mainstream way of life. It was "neither a change nor a remedy for an error."[67] Third, he ventured that the right to bear arms resides among the unalienable principles available to man. One can be deprived of it, but one cannot lose it since it was bestowed by nature. Limbaugh added that the Bill of Rights was not in any way controversial during the day of its establishment. He posed the question of whether James Madison would change his mind if he lived in the modern world. One might suppose that the Father of the Constitution would be awestruck by the types and technologies of modern weaponry available, but Limbaugh remained certain that the founder's most profound dismay would come at the sight of such a large federal government. Madison, as much as anyone else, "expected government to be oppressive."[68] In his day, it was small enough to be physically engaged and overthrown, should the need arise, leading to Limbaugh's assertion that the federal government in the 21st century would frighten the framers far more than the presence of weapons among the citizenry.

As for the dimensions of federal government, Limbaugh addressed taxation through the lens of traditional Democratic spending, paid for by raised taxes validated by Congress in cahoots with leftist administrations. He once remarked that if Thomas Jefferson thought taxation without representation was bad, "he should see it with representation."[69] In a general discussion of

---

[64] Rush Limbaugh.com

[65] Rush Limbaugh.com, A History Lesson on the Second Amendment, Oct. 6, 2017 – www.rushlimbaugh.com/daily/2017/10/06/a-history-lesson-on-the-second-amendment/

[66] Rush Limbaugh.com

[67] Rush Limbaugh.com

[68] Rush Limbaugh.com

[69] AZ Quotes

economic issues, the lines are again drawn between layman and academician. Limbaugh, like Donald Trump, has held himself out as the layman fighting the elite, self-possessed scholar. Anti-wealth taxes on the rich are anathema to his economic credo, and Limbaugh has been adamant that no one should ever apologize for making money, striving to make more of it, or fighting to keep every cent possible. Such a position is discussed daily across the country in more than 300 "Rush Rooms,"[70] set aside in restaurants and taverns across virtually every state.

LGBTQ rights, to Limbaugh, exhibit the most extreme demonstrations of political correctness at work in the nation, and he considers them part of an eventual federal takeover of private property and personal rights. In a *Huffington Post* article, he is quoted as equating the national acceptance of gay marriage to pedophilia, the normalization of dysfunction, and the "bringing [of] dark desires to light."[71] Pedophilia and gay normalcy have evolved, he said, from a crime to liberally embraced gender traits by way of intrusive government, decay of mainstream faith, and a faux-eclectic public condition that gratifies the elite with a chic image.

For his radio audience, more satire was in order. Limbaugh cited "that the difference between Los Angeles and yogurt is that yogurt comes with less fruit."[72] He joked with a caller who described himself as the only conservative in San Francisco, enjoying a mutual field day with a discussion of 72 possible genders. From there, he segued to the plight of the homeless, gleefully expressing a long-held desire to oversee the Homeless Olympics. He went on to list a series of insulting events related to life on the street. In a great "get" for the animated satire genre, Limbaugh appeared on *Family Guy* as a conservative hero breaking up a multi-racial gang attack as a martial arts wizard. The character sang, danced, and brawled, and he could even transform into a bald eagle.

Beginning in 2013, *The Adventures of Rush Revere* series was released one "adventure" at a time..Limbaugh and his wife Kathryn began the project in order to address "a void in patriotic American history in today's school system."[73] A mix of entertaining characters visited by Revere and his sidekick, Liberty, use time travel to successfully engage the imaginations of young readers. *Rush Revere and the Brave Pilgrims* came out first in 2013, with *Rush Revere and the First Patriots* available the following year. *Rush Revere and the Star-Spangled Banner* was published in 2015, with the high-selling *Rush Revere and the Presidency* following in 2016. During the collaboration, Limbaugh considered a separation from his fourth wife after a breakdown in the relationship, but he was forced to reconsider from a financial standpoint, and also due to Kathryn's deteriorating physical condition.

---

[70] David J. Haas, Lori D. Zimbleman, Harold R. Christensen, The Economic Pronouncements of Social Philosophers: Rush Limbaugh and Will Rogers, *Studies in Popular Culture,* Vol. 17 No. 2 (April 1995)

[71] Cavan Sieczkowski, Huffington Post, Rush Limbaugh Compares Gay Marriage Acceptance to Pedophilia 'Normalization' – www.huffpost.com/entry/rush-limbaugh-marriage-pedophilia-normalized_n_2431805

[72] Biography, Rush Limbaugh

[73] Rush Revere.us/The Adventures of Rush Revere – www.rushrevere.us/history

In 2017, Kathryn was accused of cheating on her husband with several younger men, including one who was married. Among her meeting places was the family's private jet. Devastated, Limbaugh began to prepare divorce proceedings, but in the absence of a prenuptial agreement, his wealth was put at great risk. Considering that Kathryn was his fourth wife, such a precaution would have seemed a natural order of business for a man with such a fortune, but he had gone without one. In the end, he banned her from the plane, hired a private detective, and eventually lived in a separate residence. In legal terms, he "turned a blind eye to her indiscretions."[74]

From the time of their early dating, Kathryn had begun to experience abdominal pain, and the condition progressed into a state of extreme fatigue. According to Limbaugh, she "cannot hold food down"[75] and is bedridden for days at a time. The two are seldom seen together, but Limbaugh noted that at their last meeting, she looked "wrinkled and gray…like death warmed over."[76] Her supermodel looks, he said, were gone, and the illness "crushed her dream"[77] of ever having children after her ovaries were removed. Her "mystery illness" has caused much speculation, including Lyme disease or even AIDS.

In March 2019, two mosques in Christchurch, New Zealand were attacked by a gunman, leaving 49 dead, and on the air, Limbaugh embraced a conspiracy theory that the massacre was actually a leftist "false flag" operation.[78] The theory, which according to Limbaugh was credible enough to defy being discounted, described a leftist extremist who wrote the manifesto, then executed the deed in order to "smear his political enemies."[79] He went on to propose the possibility that the assassin was a "liberal Green New Deal supporter,"[80] subliminally connecting the new, young, minority Congressional members to the sentiment, a group characterized by President Trump as "The Gang." Simultaneously, he tethers his ideological enemies to a campaign designed to "boost the political left and the gun control movement."[81] The power of agenda-driven political analysis was in full force as the theory moved from a baseless and far-fetched wish to part of the central story, designed to create a "reasonable doubt" among those willing to entertain the theory.

In February 2020, shortly before President Trump's State of the Union address, Limbaugh revealed that he had been given a diagnosis of advanced lung cancer. The anecdotal prognosis

---

[74] Erin Laviola, Kathryn Adams, Rush Limbaugh's Wife, 5 Fast Facts, Heavy.com, Feb/ 3, 2020 – www.heavy.com/news/2020/02/kathryn-adams-rush-limbaugh-wife/

[75] Sara Duwal, Kathryn Adams, Limbaugh, Allstar Bio, Oct. 9, 2018 – www.allstarbio.com/kathryn-adams-limbaugh-bio-age--married-net-worth

[76] Sara Duwal

[77] Sara Duwal

[78] Huffpost.com, Rush Limbaugh

[79] Daniel Moritz-Rabson, Newsweek, Rush Limbaugh Claims New Zealand Mosque Shootings Were False Flag Operation, Offers No Evidence – www,newsweek.com/rush-limbaugh-claims-mosque-attacks-false-flag-1365260

[80] Daniel Moritz-Rabson

[81] Jason Devaney, Newsmax, Rush Limbaugh Raises the Prospect that New Zealand Massacare Was False Flag Attack – www.newsmax.com/politics/newzealand/massshootings/2019/03/15/id/9072461

suggests that his odds for survival are less than half a year. Limbaugh said that he first became aware of the problem around his last birthday after experiencing shortness of breath, and he confirmed the diagnosis with two high-profile medical institutions. For a time, he considered hiding the condition, but he soon realized that there would be stretches of time away from the microphone during treatment and its debilitating effects. Sudden absences, he believed, would arouse curiosity and anxiety within his listening base, and eventually, he would be mandated to release the information to his followers.

Despite the diagnosis, Limbaugh recently signed a renewed contract with Premiere Radio Networks, intending to continue his work to any degree possible. Not only out of a sense for survival, but in terms of professional fulfillment, Limbaugh observed that the diagnosis represented one of "the most difficult days in recent memory,"[82] as his position in the conservative radio world had provided ongoing "satisfaction and happiness"[83] for much of his life.

Announcements from key media and political figures poured in to support Limbaugh after the revelation, including former Fox News commentator Megyn Kelly and Vice President Mike Pence. Fellow conservative pundit Michael Koolidge tweeted in support, addressing Limbaugh with a familiar and endearing nickname, "El Rushbo." Along with waves of support, social media was "filled with predictable waves of hatred,"[84] an indication of the country's immense political divides.

President Trump, long a close friend of Limbaugh and in some sense a phenomenon created by the radio giant, had announced his new contract with Premiere a month before. The two were not always on the same side. Remarking that the president should not possess authority over others' personal behavior, Limbaugh took exception to Trump's response to professional athletes kneeling during the national anthem at sporting events. In virtually every other category, however, they have mostly agreed as of late, and they have held numerous discussions through golf outings and regular calls. Limbaugh has personally supported Trump's presidency with an unmatched ferocity, attributing all opposition to Democrats' "pure, raw hatred"[85] for Trump's dashing of the liberal dream.

At the State of the Union Address in early February 2020, President Trump made his affections clear. Pausing the proceedings, he presented Limbaugh with the Presidential Medal of Freedom, the highest civilian honor bestowed by the United States. It was affixed around Limbaugh's neck by the First Lady, Melania Trump.

---

[82] Fox News, Brian Flood, Rush Limbaugh Announces He Has 'Advanced Lung Cancer' – www.foxnews.com/media/rush-limbaughadvanced-lung-cancer

[83] Fox News, Brian Flood

[84] Mark Davis, A Prayer for Rush Limbaugh, Feb. 4, 2020, Townhall

[85] Sandy Fitzgerald, Newsmax, Rush Limbaugh: Dems motivated by 'Raw, Pure Hatred' – www.nesmax.com/politics/rush-limbaugh-democrats/2019/12/06/id/944819

Pictures of Limbaugh receiving the Presidential Medal of Freedom

His ferocity in defending the president and heaping scorn upon GOP opponents has made Limbaugh one of the administration's most effective watchdogs. Democrats were outraged when Limbaugh received the Presidential Medal of Freedom, and two days later, Lt. Colonel Alexander Vindman was fired and escorted from the White House after testifying against the president before the House during the impeachment proceedings. Taking special exception to the testimony of Professor Pamela Karlan, who allegedly insulted the president's youngest son at the hearing, Limbaugh expressed no surprise. The academic elites, he said, are accustomed to being "so intellectually incarcerated in their ideological bubbles that they have no fear of blowback"[86] from delivering such insults.

Among the most vexing difficulties of demonizing one's opponent in any ideological war or political campaign is to see them involved in the public good. The anecdotal evidence is historically ubiquitous for controversial figures demonstrating extreme philanthropy juxtaposed to premeditated assaults, regardless of motivation. Philanthropy is in no short supply throughout the Limbaugh story. *Big League Politics* has calculated that he has personally raised over $47 million for leukemia and lymphoma research and treatment through the structure of *The Rush Limbaugh Show*. Serving as the head cheerleader at the microphone, Limbaugh personally pledged $400,000 to start a Cure-A-Thon broadcast each year. He has taken over the mortgage for a fallen police officer's family, and he supported the Stephen Siller charity, Tunnels and Towers, emphasizing the plight of firefighter families in the wake of Siller's death. In the aftermath of Nike sidelining a Betsy Ross-themed shoe, Limbaugh introduced a Betsy Ross t-shirt that earned over $2 million.

The allure of a charismatic ideologue with an enormous platform is always difficult to define at face value. One must ask which components of the "ministry" are intended as theater and ascertain the dimensions of the nugget of authenticity at the core. One must consider the degree of public demonization of a "rogue" figure weighed against real or imagined offenses committed against the well-being of his victims. To reach conclusions that are immune to flexibility is nearly impossible, as the layers of such an individual defy being peeled away for any but those in his inner circle.

Rush Limbaugh will always be an endlessly controversial figure, but everyone can agree he understood the recipe for political radio stardom. He employed a foundation present in the Will Rogers monologue that broke open the tradition of dry, scripted reporting and pushed the envelope of societal niceties. By design, political correctness was stressed to a tipping point at which the national audience had no choice but to divide into ideological camps. Adding layers of evangelical overtones to public communications, with a pinch of pop culture and stand-up comedy, Limbaugh found a far more lucrative mode of political discourse. In his carefully controlled experiment, opposition was eliminated from the citizen's mind. This replaced the moderate, understated debate of mutually adversarial politics, which beforehand moved the country forward or laterally in comparatively slow motion. Both the beneficent public servant and the tyrant have historically understood this potent manner of commanding a democracy's attention.

---

[86] David Limbaugh, Daily Wire, Limbaugh: Trump-Hating Leftists Are No Friends of the Constitution – www.dailywire.com/news/limbaugh-trump-hating-leftists-are-no-friends-of-the-constitution

Clearly, the recipe employed by Limbaugh is potent in the search to inspire, and to destroy. In league with President Trump, Limbaugh's approach to discourse is distinctly more commanding for much of the population than the academic and deliberate pursuit of ideas. The charisma of the style, whether well-informed or not, is intended to puncture "the absurd strictures of political correctness."[87] Challenging such ideologies is a mobile pursuit, as the Limbaugh model doesn't want anyone to know the ratio of ingredients. An important component of the host's image lies in preserving his role as "the merry prankster"[88] of the American right.

Jeff Schechtman has put together a better analysis than most by pointing out that ancient forms of protest are always present in such a phenomenon. In terms of direct retaliation by the sober academic world against Limbaugh, employing the same venom is singularly ineffective. One University of Miami study claims that in that all of the furor, America has been hoodwinked at every level. Limbaugh's very existence is driven by a scam reconstructed regularly for public presentation, yet when others use similar levels of vulgarity and profanity, they fail to have the desired effect or damage Limbaugh's reputation. At the same time, attempts to damage Limbaugh often flail simply because they are not as good at the forms of demagoguery he has mastered.

Even the University of Miami study's prognosis is dubious at best when it claimed that "the old fart bag is finally running out of gas."[89] To a base that views Limbaugh heroically and as a conservative Messiah, the greater likelihood is that he will continue to influence conservatism with or without a show as numerous disciples seek to carry the torch for future generations and their battles with the left.

All the while, investigations that exhibit far less "sizzle" continue to plod along. Politifact claims that 93% of Limbaugh's assertions over the years can be categorized as either "half-true, mostly false, or worse."[90] How deeply into the national consciousness such statistics will seep is difficult to predict, but Politifact's readership possesses nowhere near the dynamism of the Limbaugh "radioship."

A second analysis offered by Christopher Boyd of the Institute of General Semantics fares better than the Miami effort. Boyd, enlisting other authorities, analyzed the power of Limbaugh's use of words in *Speaking Rushian*. Boyd listed five ways in which good information is contorted and moved away from a listener's reality. The first is dubbed *Ad Hominem*, or "to the man." In this tactic, Limbaugh attacks the bearer of the message without mentioning the logic of his content. A typical example contains the phrase, "How could anything valid come from a person like this?"[91] The second strategy is called *Mind Reading*, such as found in various quotes from

---

[87] Allison Perlman

[88] Allison Perlman

[89] Michael Egan, Humor Times.com, Study Proves Rush Limbaugh Really Does Talk S**t, June 10, 2015 –
    www.humortimes.com/35411/study-rush-limbaugh-talks-shit.

[90] Michael Egan

the show ("What they're thinking is…what they really want is…"[92]). An accompanying stylistic point deals in the misuse of statistics and *Number Distortion,* the use of indistinct or hyperbolic quantities. This is typified by phrases such as "A 'bunch' of liberals, 'vast' majority…a 'stunning' number…'packed' with people."[93] Boyd likened this style of oratory to medical quackery, in which predictions are "sufficiently vague"[94] as to raise the odds of the predicted event occurring. The misuse of stats and news items are used in the same way a winning slot machine sounds the alarm in a crowded casino. Hearing the winning sound and seeing the flashing lights enhances the illusion that a rash of victories is occurring. Phrases such as "Why just today I was reading in [the newspaper]…"[95] are generally followed by "This is just another example of…"[96] Finally, it is paramount that the secular evangelist employ what is called *Think for Others*. In this arena, solutions come not from debate, but from the opposite. Limbaugh admitted freely, "The show is devoted exclusively to what I think…Callers are not allowed to read someone else's opinion, or even their own…"[97] He added as a bonus that "I'll you what to think about as well."[98] This rejection of all other sources is reflected in his own books; *The Way Things Ought to Be*, for example, lists no sources and has no citations.

In a real sense, Limbaugh is a pioneer of pamphleteering in the technological age, and his career represents a supreme achievement when it comes to influencing the conservative movement. Without him, it's fair to wonder whether Fox News would exist as it does, and if so, whether it would have such high ratings. MSNBC, CNN, and other liberal and moderate organizations sprang up in response to the corporate information powers fostered by Limbaugh's imagination. The Republican Party itself has eschewed its moderates as Trump seized the reins, using rhetoric and defying traditional norms in ways that helped establish *The Rush Limbaugh Show*. All these entities achieved a social rhythm by which one could bolster the other until the ideological cart and horse became indistinguishable.

In order to concoct the Limbaugh phenomenon, a fortuitous mix of realities was required to come together at the proper time. In the earliest attempts to recreate conservative commentary through a "right-wing Jon Stewart,"[99] neither Limbaugh nor his radio promoters had any idea how seriously he would be taken. It soon became apparent that the key to all the results lay within Limbaugh himself. His brand of humorous, angry, informed conservatism, often delivered with rhetorical reflexes worthy of Robin Williams, made him the "dean of modern radio shouters."[100] Throughout his career, he's been "a storyteller, a polemicist, an evangelist, an

---

[91] Christopher Boyd, Speaking Rushian, ETC, a Review of Semantics, Vol. 51 no. 3 (Fall 1994), *Institute of General Semantics.*

[92] Christopher Boyd

[93] Christopher Boyd

[94] Christopher Boyd

[95] Christopher Boyd

[96] Christopher Boyd

[97] Christopher Boyd

[98] Christopher Boyd

unmatched analyst…[and a] gracious, welcoming host to all who would listen,"[101] the lone exception being the liberal caller who occasionally slips through the call screening. Similarly, this juggernaut of informed research mixed with an individualistic irrationality, dubbed by followers as the "Doctor of Democracy,"[102] has reigned as a terror to non-conservatives through the nation in a timespan surpassing three decades.

Through the entire process, Limbaugh kept a tight hold on his listeners and never allowed his base to lose an iota of conservative identity. Liberalism has had its share of success through *The Colbert Report*, Jimmy Kimmel, and Jon Stewart's *Daily Show*, but Limbaugh has bestowed one clear principle upon conservative America, and it is fittingly related to a nostalgic past: "To understand the Republican Party, get in a car, turn on the radio, and drive."[103]

Online Resources

Other books about 20th century history by Charles River Editors

Other books about 21st century history by Charles River Editors

Other books about Rush Limbaugh on Amazon

Further Reading

American Conservative Union, CPAC, 2020 – www.cpac.conservative.org

AZQuotes.com, Rush Limbaugh – www.azquotes.com/author/8876-Rush_Limbaugh

Barker, David C., The Talk Radio Community: Non-traditional Social Networks and Political Participation, *Social Science Quarterly* Vol. 79 No. 2 (June 1998) University of Texas Press

Billy Binion, Rush Limbaugh Abandons Fiscal Conservatism, 18/2019 – Reason – www.reason.com/2019/07/18/rush-limbaugh-abandons-fiscal-conservatism/

Biography, Rush Limbaugh – www.biography.com/media-figure/rush-limbaugh

---

[103] Jeff Schechtman
90. Jeff Schechtman
91 Jess Schechtman
92 Who2 Biographies, Rush Limbaugh – www.who2.com/bio/rush-limbaugh
93. Mark Davis
94. Sandy Fitzgerals

Boyd, Christopher, Speaking Rushian, ETC, a Review of Semantics, Vol. 51 no. 3 (Fall 1994), *Institute of General Semantics.*

CBS News.com, Rush Limbaugh Arrested on Drug Charges, April 28, 2006 – www.cbsnews.com/news/rush-limbaugh-arrested-on-drug-charges/

Christian Forums, Politifact, 93% of Limbaugh's Claims "Half-True, False, or Worse

Claussen, Steven, Review of The Echo Chamber: Rush Limbaugh and the Conservative Media Establishment by Kathleen Hall Jamieson, Joseph N. Cappella, *Cinema Journal*, Vol. 64 No. 2 (Summer 2000) Oxford University Press

Davis, Mark, A Prayer for rush Limbaugh, Feb. 4, 2020/02/04/, Townhall – www.townhall.com/columnists/mark-davis/2020/02/04/a-prayer-for-rush-limbaugh-n2560668

Devaney, Jason Newsmax, Rush Limbaugh Raises the Prospect that New Zealand Massacare Was False Flag Attack – www.newsmax.com/politics/newzealand/massshootings/2019/03/15/id/9072461

Encyclopaedia Britannica, Rush Limbaugh, American Radio Personality and Author, Jan. 8, 2020-www.britannica.com/biography/Rush-Limbaugh

Egan, Michael, Study Proves Rush Limbaugh Really Does Talk S**t, Humor Timnes.com, June 10, 2015 – www.humortimes.com/35411/study-ruwsh-limbaugh-talks-shit/

Fitzgerald, Sandy, Rush Limbaugh: Dems Motivated by 'Pure, Raw Hatred – www.newsmax.com/politics/rush-limbaugh-democrats/2019/12/06/id/944819/

Flood, Brian, Rush Limbaugh Announces He Has 'Advanced Lung Cancer' – www.foxnews.com/media/rush-limbaugh-advanced-lung-cancer

Fox News.com, Associated Press, Rush Limbaugh Felt 'Heart Attack Coming On', Jan. 1, 2010 – www.foxnews.com/story/rush-limbaugh-felt-heart-attack-coming-on

Goodreads.com, The Way Things Ought to Be – www.goodreads.com/book/show/543707.The_Way_Things_Ought_to_Be

Haas, David J., Zimbleman, Lori, Christensen, Harold R., The Economic Pronouncements of Social Philosophers: Rush Limbaugh and Will Rogers, *Studies in Popular Culture*, Vol. 17 No. 2 (April, 1995)

History-biography, Rush Limbaugh, March 8, 2019 – www.history-biography.com/rush-limbaugh/

Huffpost.com, Rush Limbaugh – www.huffpost.com/news/topic/rush-limbaugh

I Heart Radio, Why Would the Obamas Buy a Doomed Beach House? Premiere Networks, Aug. 23, 2019 – www.iheart.com/featured/rush-limbaugh/content/2019-08-23-pn-n-l-why-wouold-the-obamas-buy-a-doomed-beachhouse/

IMDB, Biography, Rush Limbaugh.com – www.imdb.com/name/nm0510754/bio

IMDB.com, The ½ Half Hour News Hour – www.imdb.com/title/tt0887788/

Information Cradle, Rush Limbaugh – www.informatioincradle.com/rush-limbaugh/

KFGW, Rush Limbaugh – www.player.listenlive.com/35131/en/show/1

Lake, Frank, Rush Limbaugh Fired, Weekly World News, March 6, 2012 – www.weeklyworldnews.com/headlines/44895/rush-limbaugh-fired

Laviola, Erin, Kathryn Adams, Rush Limbaugh's Wife, 5 Fast Fact. News Talk 1290, Rush Limbaugh – Live – www.heavy.com/news/2020/02.kathryn-adams-rush-limbaugh-wife/

Limbaugh, David, Daily Wire, Limbaugh: Trump-Hating Leftists Are No Friends of the Constitution – wqww.dailywire.com/news/Limbaugh-trump-hating-leftists-are-no-friends-of-the-constitution

Luckowski, James, Lopach, james J., Critical Thinking about Political Commentary, *Journal of Adolescent & Adult Literacy,* Vol. 44 no. 3 (Nov 2000)

Martin, Amy, Review : Rush Limbaugh in Night School – www.moonlady.com/review-rush-limbaugh-in-night-school/

MediaMatters for America, Echoing Glenn Beck, Rush Limbaugh Mocks Malia Obama – www.mediamatters.org/echoing-glenn-beck-rush-limbaugh-mocks-Malia-Obama

Moritz-Rabson,, Daniel, Newsweek, Rush Limbaugh Claims New Zealand Mosque Shootings Were False Flag Operation, Offers No Evidence – www,newsweek.com/rush-limbaugh-claims-mosque-attacks-false-flag-1365260

National Geographic, August 4, 1987, CE: Fairness Doctrine Repealed – www.nationalgeographic.org/thisday/aug4/fairness-doctrine-repealed

News Talk 1290.com/Limbaugh-and-fluke-the-not-so-love-story

Perlman, Allison, Rush Limbau and the Problem of the Color Line, *Cinema Journal*, Vol. 51 No. 4 (Summer 2012) University of Texas

Reed, Anna, Puente Puente, Rush Limbaugh Reveals Lung Cancer Diagnosis, USA Today, Yahoo Entertainment, Megyn Kelly Sends Support, Feb. 3, 2020 – www.yahoo.com/rush-limbaugh-reveals-advanced-lung-202404452.html

Rush Limbaugh: The Master of Racial; Passion, *Journal of Blacks in Higher Education* No. 64 (Summer 2009) JBHE Foundation

Rush Revere.us, Adventures of Rush Revere – www.rushrevere.us/history

Schechtman, Jeff, The Mouth That Roared, How Rush Limbaugh Changed America, Who What Why – www.whowhatwhy.org/2018/08/07/the-mouth-that-roared-how-rush-limbaugh-changed-america/

Sieczkowski, Cavan, Huffington Post, Rush Limbaugh Compares Gay Marriage Acceptance to Pedophilia 'Normalization' – www,huffpost.com/entry/rush-limbaugh-marriage-pedophilia-normalized_n_2431805

Simpson, Andrea, National Enquirer, Nov. 24, 2015 – www.nationalenquirer.com/celebrity/why-rush-limbaugh-no-rush-divorce-his-sick-wife/

The Famous People, Rush Limbaugh – www.thefamouspeoploe.com/profiles/rush-hudson-limbaugh-iii-2772.php

Tulsa's News and Talk, 102.3 KRMG, Rush Limbaugh – www.krmg.com/entertainment/personalities/shows/rush-limbaugh/

Who2Biogrraphies, Rush Limbaugh – www.Who2.com/bio/rush-limbaugh/

WMAL, 105.9 FM, Rush Limbaugh – www.wmal.com/rush-limbaugh/

Free Books by Charles River Editors

We have brand new titles available for free most days of the week. To see which of our titles are currently free, click on this link.

Discounted Books by Charles River Editors

We have titles at a discount price of just 99 cents everyday. To see which of our titles are currently 99 cents, click on this link.